RED STAR
TO HEYBROOK BAY

The story of J.W. Newton and Sons
(Star Motors) and
the Heybrook Bay Motor Services Ltd

by Roger Grimley

Cover picture:
Pictured at the East Street terminus in Plymouth in the early post-war years is CDR 780, a Heybrook Bay Motor Services Bedford built to utility standards. Behind the vehicle can be seen the sites of buildings destroyed in the blitz and which became part of the Royal Parade development. (East Pennine Transport Group - R. Marshall collection)

ISBN No. 1 872863 04 3

Published by Kithead Ltd in conjunction with Roger Grimley at De Salis Drive, Hampton Lovett, Droitwich Spa, Worcs, WR9 0QE

Preface

The advent of motor transport and the coming of the country 'bus contributed to one of the greatest changes in rural society to have come about in one man's lifetime. Instead of being part of a largely self-contained community, villagers were able to travel easily and regularly to the nearest market town or to go on outings to the seaside or moors. Their world changed and at no time was the pace of change as great as during the 1920's.

The first part of this book is a record of the life and times of J. W. NEWTON & SONS ("STAR MOTOR SERVICE") and incorporates the recollections of members of the Newton family -- Elsie Hudson, Ivy Bone and John Newton. It came about as the result of the interest and encouragement of Jenny Wakeling, the grand-daughter of Bill Newton.

It is the story of one man who, after suffering an injury during army service in India, came to Devon. Losing both his job and the house that went with it upon the death of his employer, he saw an opportunity to make a living conveying people between the area to the east of Plymouth Sound and the city.

In spite of considerable difficulties he built up the Star Motors to be a familiar part of everyday life for the inhabitants of Heybrook Bay, Down Thomas, Staddiscombe, Elburton, Billacombe and Plymouth. His 'buses took people to work, to the market and shops, to the cinema or theatre for entertainment, to the doctor or hospital in times of need. They brought city dwellers out from war ravaged Plymouth to the relative safety of the countryside during their time of trial. They carried not only people but parcels and provided a friendly, personal and reliable service, known locally as the "Red Star".

The second part covers the post war years when the business was continued by the Hart family under the title HEYBROOK BAY MOTOR SERVICES LTD. The help given by Mrs Peggy Hart is gratefully acknowledged.

Thanks are also due to the P.S.V. Circle, Geoff Bruce, Bob Crawley, John Madge, Mike Parsons and others who, over the years, have made their records available.

Photographs from the Newton family and Heybrook Bay Motor Services have been supplemented by others from A.B.Cross and the East Pennine Transport Group (R. Marshall collection), to whom thanks are due.

Many of the photographs were taken between sixty and seventy years ago.   Some of the prints were damaged or faded and may not reproduce to the standard we would have liked.   However, because of their particular relevance and historical interest they have been included.

Also, my love and gratitude to Barbara Grimley for all her patience, encouragement and practical help in libraries, record offices and through the highways and byways of Devon during the last forty years.

Roger Grimley

Coddington
May,1993

Chapter One : The Early Years.

James William (Bill) Newton hailed from Nottingham. On leaving school he started work in a coal mine, leading the blind pit ponies who pulled the coal wagons between the coal face and the bottom of the pit shaft. This must have been a hard existence for a twelve year old child.

At the age of fourteen, because of conditions at home, he ran away and joined the army but was fetched back by his mother. Not long after, she died and so Bill returned to the army, joining the Sherwood Foresters as a drummer boy. Later he became a regular soldier but, while serving in India before the First World War, was shot in the knee during a skirmish in Bangalore and was invalided home.

He spent several years in and out of hospital, after each spell trying to pick up the threads and find work. He married, children started arriving, and he and his wife kept a greengrocery shop in Chesterfield. It is also believed that he worked as a 'bus driver in the area for a time.

After another stay in hospital Bill Newton and his family moved to Ivybridge, in Devon, where they had a general store. He still experienced considerable trouble with his leg which meant going into Kings College Hospital in London, where consideration was given to amputation. His leg was saved by an American surgeon who was passing through London. However, with three small children to care for, the shop had to go so he found employment at Loddiswell, near Kingsbridge, where the family lived at Woolston Lodge.

In 1919 the post of chauffeur to Doctor Clay of Wembury House, near Plymouth, was obtained and the Newton family moved to accommodation provided with the job at the Lodge in the grounds. After three years service disaster befell the family when Doctor Clay died and Bill found himself out of work with one weeks notice to leave the house in which he and his family lived. Most of the family possessions had to be sold and Bill spent many hours on his motor-bike scouring the countryside for somewhere to live. Eventually he managed to rent two rooms behind Mr George Avery's shoe repair shop at nearby Down Thomas and in these he set up home again with his wife and then four children.

THE WEMBURY ROUTE

The next question was how to make a living. During his time with Doctor Clay, Bill Newton had seen Wembury people walking the two miles or more to Elburton, where they caught the Great Western Railway motor-buses running between Kingsbridge and Plymouth. On the return journey heavy shopping had to be carried over a hilly road home. The only public transport was that provided by the Plymouth char-a-banc proprietors and which catered mainly for Plymouth people going out to the popular beach at Wembury during the summer months.

His previous experience as a 'bus driver in Chesterfield may have been in his mind when, in December, 1922, Bill Newton decided to enter the motor-bus business. He scraped together enough money to buy a vehicle but the sale fell through and he had to borrow £20 from his mother-in-law, later repaid, to purchase a second-hand Model 'T' Ford fitted with a 'sit-up-and-beg' type open-sided body. Accommodation for fourteen passengers was on benches arranged along the sides of the body and there were canvas curtains which could be drawn across in bad weather.

The Ford was used to start a regular motor-bus service between Wembury, Elburton and Plymouth. This ran on Tuesdays, Thursdays and Saturdays - market days. The Plymouth terminus was at the Norley Yard, off Ebrington Street, and was shared with other carriers running in from many of the villages in the surrounding countryside.

Newton's service allowed village folk to go into Plymouth for shopping, for entertainment or just to see the sights of the big town. During the summer it competed for traffic from Plymouth to the beach below Wembury village and at holiday times as many journeys as possible were run out of Plymouth in the morning. Life in those days was a struggle and every opportunity had to be taken to increase the takings. Before the last trip out in the morning Bill Newton would purchase a consignment of ice cream and this he would sell on the beach until it was time to start taking people back into town in the late afternoon.

During the summer of 1923 there was rivalry with the Plymouth char-a-banc owners for the pleasure traffic but by August of that year a far more formidable competitor appeared. The Devon Motor Transport Co. Ltd. (DMT) had started in Okehampton immediately after the First World War. It expanded rapidly and a depot was established in Plymouth during 1922. DMT 'buses were soon operating between Plymouth and Ermington via Elburton then additional journeys were introduced to and from Wembury, running over Bill Newton's route five times every weekday and four times on Sundays.

At the end of the 1923 season DMT withdrew from the Wembury route but resumed again for the summer of 1924, with five return trips every day. They then decided to eliminate the competition and started "nursing" Bill Newton's 'bus. One DMT vehicle would run immediately in front of him, with another just behind. As a one-man business he found it hard to compete with the larger company which had greater resources and more luxurious vehicles. When, finally, his fares were undercut Mr Newton was forced off the Wembury - Plymouth route.

DEVON MOTOR TRANSPORT CO.LTD
Time Table : Plymouth to Wembury via Elburton : August, 1923

	Weekdays					Sundays			
	am	pm	pm	pm	pm	am	pm	pm	pm
Plymouth	9.05	12.15	2.30	5.20	7.15	10.30	2.00	5.20	7.15
Wembury	9.50	1.00	3.15	6.05	8.00	11.15	2.45	6.05	8.00
	am	pm	pm	pm	pm	am	pm	pm	pm
Wembury	10.00	1.45	3.20	6.10	8.15	11.16	3.00	6.10	8.15
Plymouth	10.45	2.29	4.05	6.55	9.00	12.00	3.45	6.55	9.00

THE DOWN THOMAS SERVICE

Although he had suffered financially as a result of the battle with the DMT, Bill Newton sought a new opportunity for a 'bus service.

The small settlements of Down Thomas, where he lived, and Staddiscombe were unserved by 'bus so he re-established himself by opening up a new route into Plymouth. This served Down Thomas, Staddiscombe, Elburton and Plymouth twice every Tuesday and Thursday and three times on Saturday. Between Elburton and Plymouth it competed with the Great Western Railway and DMT 'buses as well as those of several small operators.

Mr Newton kept a book in which he recorded each passenger by name and also noted each parcel carried, listed by recipients name and address. Expenses at first included the toll payable for crossing Laira Bridge but this was later abolished.

Some of his former passengers were very loyal. After the Down Thomas route was started Mrs Dixon, the elderly schoolmistress at Wembury, would walk the hilly road to Ridge Cross to catch Bill Newton's 'bus to Plymouth rather than ride on the DMT from her home village. There were other regular passengers. Among them were Mr Giles of Princes Farm, Down Thomas, who always went to Plymouth on Saturdays. Another was Miss Gaunt, who had a stall in Plymouth Market Square and sent sweets for the Newton children every Saturday.

The early days on the Down Thomas route were a continual struggle, particularly during the winter when there were no town dwellers riding out to Down Thomas, whence they walked down the rough track to Bovisand Bay. This destination grew in popularity over the years and several shops and tea-rooms were opened. There were also changing huts on the beach and several stalls selling "pop", etc. Harold and Albert Newton worked at some of these during the school holidays, as did some other local boys.

A local guide for the 1930's reads:-
"Bovisand Beach.......is a favourite resort of picnickers, as it is easily accessible by motor-boats from Plymouth, Devonport and Stonehouse alike. There are good sands and several quiet bays with facilities for bathing, while light refreshments may be obtained in the tea huts and cottages."

Other work was obtained for the 'bus. Private parties were carried, such as the Boys Brigade and Girl Guides to camp at Heybrook Bay and Bovisand. The youngsters from the National Childrens Home were taken to the beach once a year and local people were conveyed on trips over the moors and to Plymouth Carnival.

The original Model 'T' was replaced by another second-hand Ford. This second vehicle appears to have had a relatively short life with Mr Newton and was superseded by a Morris-Commercial 'bus bought from the Links Hotel at Thurlestone. This had an upright saloon body with doors at the front and rear reached by steps. An iron ladder at the back of the vehicle gave access to parcel and luggage space on the roof. The side of the 'bus was lettered "Down Thomas - Elburton - Plymouth".

By 1928 three round trips were run to Plymouth each Tuesday, Thursday and Saturday. The return journeys left Plymouth at 1 p.m., 4 p.m. and 7 p.m. with the terminus now situated in East Street, near the Corn Exchange. Local directories also show a Friday service leaving Plymouth Corn Exchange at 4 p.m. for Wembury, Staddiscombe and Down Thomas but the accuracy of this has not been confirmed.

In about 1925 a piece of land at Down Thomas had been bought and on this Bill Newton built his first garage. Behind it he erected a wooden bungalow in which to live with his wife and six children. The bricks for the foundations and the wooden sections for the house were from old army huts at Heybrook Bay and were transported back to Down Thomas on the 'bus. In succeeding years a second small garage was added at a cost of £25, then during 1932-1935 the original garage was replaced by a newer structure at a total cost of £118.10.4d.

SCHOOL CONTRACTS

By 1930 Devon County Council were centralizing senior school education, leaving many village schools to cater only for infants and juniors. In pursuance of this policy the older pupils at Wembury School were transferred to Plymstock Senior School as from 1st April, 1930. The Council agreed to provide transport for those living in the Down Thomas and Wembury areas and Mr Newton's tender of 10/- per day for the hire of a coach (soon raised to 12/-) was accepted.

However, a problem soon arose as a result of Bill Newton's practice of letting the young children from Down Thomas ride to and from Wembury School, which he passed en route. Even though there were empty seats on this section the County Council objected, not wishing to create a precedent by carrying children who were not eligible for free transport. As a result Mr Newton gave notice to terminate the contract.

A new operator was sought but none was forthcoming. Therefore, an agreement was reached by which Mr Newton continued to operate the route and the infants and juniors were allowed to ride on the 'bus provided for the senior children. This saved the younger pupils a long walk after which they had often arrived at school soaking wet. From 1932 the County Council paid Mr Newton £1 per day, a rate which continued until wartime conditions caused it to be increased by ten per cent.

H.902.

By Messrs. **J. W. Newton and Son** ("Star" Motor Service), of Downthomas, near Plymouth, for a Road Service Licence to continue the service of stage·carriages between Heybrook Bay and Plymouth, via Downthomas, Staddiscombe, Elburton and Billacombe.

Modification :—

The Summer time schedule to be revised as follows :—

X.

		a.m.	a.m.	a.m.	a.m.	p.m.
Heybrook Lodge	dep.	8.0	9.25	10.55	—	12.25
Downthomas ..	,,	8.5	9.30	11.0	11.30	12.30
Plymouth ..	arr.	8.30	9.55	11.25	11.55	12.55
Plymouth ..	dep.	8.40	10.10	11.40	12.10	1.10
Downthomas ..	arr.	9.6	10.36	12.6	12.36	1.36
Heybrook Lodge	,,	9.10	10.40	12.10	12.40	1.40

K.

		p.m.	p.m.	p.m.	p.m.	p.m.	p.m.
Heybrook Lodge	dep.	1.55	3.25	5.25	6.25	8.25	—
Downthomas ..	,,	2.0	3.30	5.30	7.0	8.30	9.5
Plymouth ..	arr.	2.25	3.55	5.55	7.25	8.55	9.30
Plymouth ..	dep.	2.40	4.10	6.10	7.40	9.10	9.40
Downthomas ..	arr.	3.6	4.36	6.36	8.6	9.36	10.6
Heybrook Lodge	,,	3.10	4.40	6.40	8.10	9.40	—

X Not Sundays.   K Saturdays and Sundays only.

Heybrook Bay-Plymouth summer timetable 1933
(Western T.A. N&P 29th May 1933)

Chapter Two : Star Motors

In the late 1920's and during the 'thirties a developer erected houses on the cliffs at Heybrook Bay, overlooking the entrance to Plymouth Sound. By 1930 Mr Newton had extended his Plymouth service some three-quarters of a mile beyond Down Thomas to terminate at Heybrook Lodge.

To meet the demands of the growing population the service ran at intervals of about one and a half hours daily. On Weekdays the first 'bus was at 8 a.m. and the last at 8 p.m., but on Sundays the start was delayed until 9.30 a.m. Between Elburton and Plymouth the main competitor was now the Western National Omnibus Co. Ltd. This company had been formed in 1929 to take over the routes operated by the National Omnibus & Transport Co. Ltd, which had acquired the Devon Motor Transport and the operation of the Great Western Railway's motor-bus services. There were also the "Zenith" 'buses of Evan Lowe until they, too, were acquired by Western National in 1933.

To cover the extended routes and daily operation of the Plymouth service, as well as the contract to carry schoolchildren, the Morris-Commercial was joined by a fourteen-seater Chevrolet in January, 1931. This was the first brand new 'bus for the business and was registered DR 7888.

Both 'buses were painted a light shade of navy blue on the bottom half, red on the top half. The roof and lettering were white with a gold star on the side panels (and in later years on the rear). The name "Star Motor Service" was adopted but locally they were usually referred to as the "Red Star".

Because of Bill Newton's injured leg he found it difficult to operate both foot brake and accelerator, so the controls on his 'bus were modified to include a hand operated throttle. Ernie Harwood was employed as a driver and he was soon joined by Jack Ash as conductor. Elsie Newton left school at the age of thirteen to become her father's secretary.

With the employment of staff, tickets were introduced. Different colours were used for each value and a long white ticket with an over-printed cross was given to passengers in exchange for return tickets handed in. The firm of Williamson of Ashton-under-Lyne supplied both the tickets and the waybills on which details of issues and receipts were recorded for each journey. For passengers carried within the City of Plymouth special tickets, obtained from the City Treasurer's Office at the Guildhall, were issued and a percentage of the fare was paid to the Corporation. Ticket punches were used and the small, round pieces of paper punched out of the tickets made good confetti at weddings.

When traffic was heavy, or if Bill Newton wanted a break, vehicles would be hired from Mr Albert Rodgman of Pomphlet, who ran the "Violet Cars" and had built bodies for some of the early local chars-a-banc, or from Mrs Williams of the Embankment Motor Company in Plymouth.

ROAD TRAFFIC ACT

The implementation of the Road Traffic Act in 1931 brought a system of licensing for all 'bus routes, vehicles and staff which replaced a variety of local council regulations. It severely restricted new entrants and bestowed upon licence holders an assurance that they could not easily be challenged.

Mr Newton was authorized to continue the daily service between Heybrook Lodge and Plymouth (under Traffic Commissioners reference H902) and the two 'buses received Public Service Vehicle licences.

With the threat of additional competition now reduced, a new Bedford 'bus was bought in November, 1931. This make had been introduced a few months earlier and was proving very popular. It had 20 seats, was registered DR 9379 and its arrival allowed the Morris-Commercial, now five years old, to be sold to a Cornish operator.

The hard work of the early years was now beginning to pay dividends and Bill Newton's two eldest sons were taken into partnership. Neither Albert nor Harold were involved in the day-to-day running of the business at this time as both were serving soldiers, having joined up at 16 and 14 years of age respectively.

By 1933 the fleet of J.W. Newton & Sons consisted of two 'buses and two cars. There was a Chevrolet 14-seater (DR 7888), a Bedford 20-seater (DR 9379), a Chevrolet used as a taxi and a Morris car. The 'buses were washed by Bill, his children and the drivers at the village pump, which was the main water supply for the community of Down Thomas.

During the summer months one 'bus covered the Plymouth service between 8 a.m. and 9.40 p.m., with the second 'bus needed for a round trip in and out of Plymouth at 11.30 a.m. and a late journey on Saturdays and Sundays. It also operated the school runs. During the winter a slightly reduced service was maintained.

In the previous year fares to and from Plymouth had been fixed at:-

Heybrook Bay	......	1/- Single, 1/8 Return
Down Thomas	....	10d Single, 1/4 Return

at which level they remained for many years. Weekly tickets, at slightly reduced prices, were later introduced for the benefit of people travelling to work in Plymouth each day. These tickets were about double the size of other tickets and were blue in colour.

HOLIDAY CAMPS

With paid annual holidays becoming more usual, two holiday camps were developed on the cliffs between Heybrook Bay and Wembury. There was the Lido, run by Mrs Beaumont and Eric Lancaster and, on the opposite side of the road, Wembury Point Holiday Camp. The latter was started by the Stansell family but also involved was a Mr Tom Hart of London, of whom we shall hear more later in the story.

When it was learned that Western National were interested in conveying patrons to and from Plymouth, Mr Newton stepped in quickly and in the autumn of 1934 he was granted a licence for a service which linked the camps with his Plymouth service 'buses, connecting at Rack Corner between Down Thomas and Staddiscombe. The link service ran daily from June 1st until September 30th, ending ten days earlier in subsequent years.

To cope with this extra seasonal traffic the fleet strength was increased by one during 1935. The Chevrolet, DR 7888, was sold and replaced by two vehicles. The first, which arrived on June 19th, was a second-hand 14-seater Chevrolet bought for £75. The second was a brand new Bedford, registered JY 6332 during July and which entered service on August 1st. With a larger fleet to be housed, the smaller garage at Down Thomas was improved at a cost of £15.

Visitors travelling by train from various parts of the country destined for the holiday camps would arrive at North Road Station, Plymouth. They would then have to walk to the end of the Station Approach to catch a Corporation 'bus into the centre of the city. There would then be another walk to East Street to catch the Star Motors 'bus. A further change on to the feeder service was necessary before reaching the holiday destination and each time luggage had to be handled. In order to provide more convenient facilities Newton & Sons proposed that from 1937 the connecting service should be extended on Saturdays only, with two journeys continuing on to and from Plymouth. The idea was to follow the Plymouth service route to East Street, then go via Coburg Street to North Road Station. On the return journey the 'bus would travel via York Street and Cornwall Street to reach East Street, then on to the camps. However, the application brought objections from both the Plymouth Corporation and Western National so permission was not forthcoming. Therefore, the connecting 'buses continued to run between the Camps and Rack Corner.

However Bill Newton was not content to let the matter rest and applied again, this time for a direct run between the Camps and North Road Station, with a flat fare of one shilling single. In July, 1938 this was granted and a licence was issued covering three round trips each Saturday during the season. Thereafter, the daily feeder service to and from Rack Corner continued, supplemented by the Camp - Station direct service on summer Saturdays, until the outbreak of war in 1939.

DAY-BY-DAY

The daily operation of the service was not without incident. Elsie Hudson (née Newton) recalls an occasion when her parents were taking a well-earned and much needed few days holiday in mid-summer. Mr Harry Wickens, the local Ministry of Transport vehicle examiner, arrived out of the blue and having inspected the three 'buses left a list of jobs to be done on them immediately. Panic stations ensued but the staff rallied round and worked all night with two of her brothers while Elsie cooked sausages, eggs and beans for everyone at midnight. All the work was completed by morning and the Star Motors rolled again to serve the passengers.

Each year, just before Christmas, a couple of crates of oranges would be brought out on the 'bus from Plymouth and the Newton children would go round the village selling them. A regular run on Christmas Day was to Home Park, Plymouth when Plymouth Argyle Football Club were playing at home. Mrs Newton would cook Christmas dinner for all the staff.

14

On the Elburton-Billacombe-Plymouth section of route Newton's Star Motors were greatly outnumbered by Western National 'buses running to and from the River Yealm, Noss Mayo, Kingsbridge, Dartmouth and other destinations. However, many passengers preferred the personal service of the smaller concern and would wave the National 'buses past and wait for what they called the 'Red Star'. There were no official stops along the Star Motors route and passengers would be put down outside their own front doors as often as not. The conductor would just give the driver the name of the passenger or of the house and he would stop the 'bus at the right place.

Some local people were fond of shooting and took their gun dogs with them on the 'bus. One party in particular had a lot of dogs and when paying the fares one day it was noticed that it cost more for the animals than for the people. A deal was struck with a discount given for the quantity of animals.

One man, living next to the garage in Down Thomas, worked in an ironmongers shop near Laira Bridge and his dinner was sent to him each day on the 'bus. The conveyance of packages was an important part of the business with the usual charge being threepence. Again a personal service was offered with one customer having meat delivered. It had to be left in the outside toilet to be safe from the cat!

On fine summer days there was heavy passenger traffic out of Plymouth to the coast. It was spread out over the morning journeys and with duplication the small fleet coped. However, in the evening everyone wanted to stay by the sea as long as possible and to go home at the same time. There was a mass tramp up the track from Bovisand to the edge of Down Thomas village, but by the time the 'bus got there it was often full of people who had spent the day at Heybrook Bay. So most of the passengers walked down to the Star Garage in the hope that they could catch a 'bus there. The family would come out of the bungalow, all available 'buses would be loaded and they would set off for Plymouth, taking as many as the fleet would hold. Those left behind would be given tea or cocoa by Mrs Newton until the 'buses got back from Plymouth for another load and eventually everyone got home.

CLOUDS OF WAR

In 1937 Mr and Mrs Newton's eldest son, Albert, finished his army service and joined the day-to-day operation of the business. However, sadly, their second son, Harold, was killed in an accident while serving in the army at Aldershot and this was a bitter blow to his parents.

The 'bus fleet grew to four with the purchase of another 20-seater Bedford in January 1937 at a cost of £689.10.6d. brand new. In the following summer a larger vehicle of the same make was bought. This was a 24-seater but at £669.10.0d. it actually cost less. Two cars, a Chevrolet registered DV 1138 and used as a taxi, and a Talbot, the latter bought for £45, were also owned.

Relations with the Western National company were generally cordial and the Newton family had a firm liking and respect for the local Area Traffic Superintendent, Mr Day. However, the two firms faced each other in a friendly battle across the traffic court when J.W. Newton & Son opposed an application to divert the Western National Plymouth-Wembury route away from Springfield Road, Elburton to run via Wembury Road, a section of road previously covered only by the Star Motors.

Both sides had their case presented by solicitors. Only Bill Newton gave evidence for his firm but Western National called three witnesses to speak before the Traffic Commissioners, under the chairmanship of Mr Nicholson at Plymouth Guildhall. One was Commander Abel, who got up and said that had he known his old friend Bill Newton was involved he would never have consented to speak. Another was Mr Roper from Wembury, who spoke up on Mr Newton's behalf. The Commissioners retired to consider their verdict and came back to say that they would allow Western National to divert their service but they had never heard a fairer objector than Mr Newton. If it was found that the alteration damaged his service he could come back to them and they would reconsider their decision.

Western National made several attempts to buy out the Star Motors service over the years but, although tempted at times, Mr Newton kept his independence.

At the beginning of 1939 Western National applied to run an express coach service between London and the holiday camps at Wembury Point. However, an objection by Mr Newton prevented this. Soon the larger company experienced difficulties with their staff over wage rates. A top rate of one shilling and fourpence halfpenny per hour for drivers, one shilling and twopence for conductors, was asked for but refused. As a result Plymouth depot staff came out on strike and this spread to other garages in the West Country. For a fortnight from 1st May, 1939 there were no Western National 'buses on the road and this left only the Star Motors to carry people between Elburton, Billacombe and Plymouth. Every available 'bus and member of staff was pressed into service, with extra journeys run over the above section of route.

The bungalow behind the Star Garage which Bill Newton built himself. He is seen with his sons, Albert, Harold and John, his wife Bertha and Shep the dog. Chickens and a pig were kept in the garden and these, together with flowers and blackcurrants, were sold locally to bring in extra income while the 'bus service was being built up. Furniture, pictures and china were bought at auctions and then resold, often to young married couples just setting up home.

Star Garage, Down Thomas, photographed in 1950 while it was being run by John and Arthur Newton. A Vauxhall car is in the doorway and a three-wheel Morgan can be seen between the two buildings.

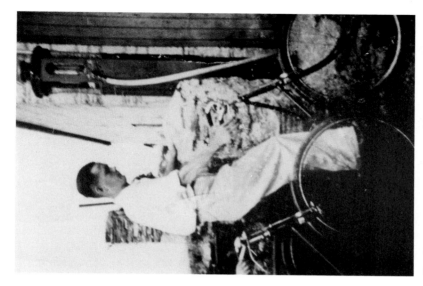

Harold Newton pictured about a year before his death in a road accident on 15th November, 1937, at the age of twenty-two. He was a Lance-Corporal in the Royal Engineers.

Albert Newton takes a break for a "cuppa" while working in the Star Motors business before the outbreak of the Second World War. He died on 18th February, 1944, from wounds received while serving with the Royal Engineers in Italy; he was then thirty years old.

John and Arthur Newton, the two youngest sons of Bill and Bertha Newton. In post-war years, after the sale of the 'bus business, they ran the garage, petrol sales and car hire business from the Star Garage, Down Thomas.

Sisters, Elsie and Ivy Newton (later Mrs Hudson and Mrs Bone) outside Star Garage in 1938. Bill Newton stored paraffin in a tank for sale to campers.

Star Garage in 1952 after the premises had been refurbished. Later the garage passed to John Beney, son-in-law of Cis Wright (née Labron) who was at one time a Star Motors conductress.

Bill Newton is seen here with his foot on the running-board of his first 'bus, the model "T" Ford which he bought in 1922. Behind him is Mr Johnnie Keen, an old soldier and well-liked member of the Wembury Point community. On the right of the picture are members of the Boys' Brigade. Marked on the windscreen is 'Bovisand Beach' although passengers were actually dropped off at the top of the lane leading down from Down Thomas to the bay.

TT 7840, the Morris 'bus purchased during the 1920's. Mrs Newton's sister, Mary Anne Taylor, always known as "Aunt Polly", is standing on the step to the rear entrance. Note the iron ladder which gave access to the roof where parcels and luggage were carried.

Chevrolet DR 7888; this was also lettered "Down Thomas-Elburton-Plymouth" on the side panels immediately below the windows. The nearside windscreen has signs Billacombe, Elburton, Staddiscombe, Down Thomas and the destination blind reads Heybrooke Bay. The final 'e' in Heybrooke was later dropped.

A 1930's view of a 'bus on the Plymouth service. The lady sitting at the back wearing a hat is Mrs Bertha Newton.

The scene at Plymstock Station when a lorry collided with JY 6332. A policeman and an A.A. Scout are in attendance as are numerous local people. Behind can be seen the roof of a second Star Motors 'bus and the railway line is the Southern branch to Turnchapel.

The road staff now included Elsie Newton, who with the threat of war and the possibility of male staff being called up for service in the armed forces, had obtained a conductor's licence in March, 1939 at the age of twenty-two. One small boy's reaction on seeing a female conductor for the first time was "Oh! look, a lady be the ticket man". Another reaction was from a regular passenger who each evening rode from his home to the Elburton Hotel, returning a couple of trips later after he had imbibed. He presented Elsie with a bottle of beer but, on being told that she did not like beer, appeared the next evening with a gin and tonic. Other passengers brought gifts for the drivers and conductors. These included birds from the shooting parties, crab apples, and flowers.

H.902.—Messrs. J. W. Newton and Son (" Star " Motor Service), of Downthomas, near Plymouth between **Heybrook Bay** and **Plymouth**, via Down Thomas, Langdon Court, Staddiscombe, Elburton and Billacombe. Modifications :—Revised Summer time-table as follows :—

		X.										K.
		a.m.	a.m.	a m.	p.m.	p.m.	p.m.	p.m.	p.m.	p.m.	p.m.	p.m.
Heybrook Lodge	dep.	8.0	9.20	10.40	12.0	2.0	3.20	4.40	6.0	7.20	8.40	—
Downthomas ..	,,	8.5	9.25	10.45	12.5	2.5	3.25	4.45	6.5	7.25	8.45	10.0
Staddiscombe ..	,,	8.10	9.30	10.50	12.10	2.10	3.30	4.50	6.10	7.30	8.50	10.5
Elburton ..	,,	8.15	9.35	10.55	12.15	2.15	3.35	4.55	6.15	7.35	8.55	10.10
Billacombe ..	,,	8.18	9.38	10.58	12.18	2.18	3.38	4.58	6.18	7.38	8.58	10.13
Plymouth ..	arr.	8.30	9.50	11.10	12.30	2.30	3.50	5.10	6.30	7.50	9.10	10.25

		X.									A.	K.
		a.m.	a.m.	a.m.	p.m.	p.m.	p.m.	p.m.	p.m.	p.m.	p.m.	p.m.
Plymouth ..	dep.	8.40	10.0	11.20	12.40	2.40	4.0	5.20	6.40	8.0	9.20	10.35
Billacombe ..	,,	8.52	10.12	11.32	12.52	2.52	4.12	5.32	6.52	8.12	9.32	10.47
Elburton ..	,,	8.55	10.15	11.35	12.55	2.55	4.15	5.35	6.55	8.15	9.35	10.50
Staddiscombe ..	,,	9.1	10.21	11.41	1.1	3.1	4.21	5 41	7.1	8.21	9.41	10.56
Downthomas ..	,,	9.6	10.26	11.46	1.6	3.6	4.26	5.46	7.6	8.26	9.46	11.1
Heybrook Lodge	arr.	9.10	10.30	11.50	1.10	3.10	4.30	5.50	7.10	8.30	9.50	—

X.—Not Sundays. K.—Downthomas, Saturdays and Sundays only. A.—Downthomas only, except Saturdays.
If the licence applied for under Application H.4899 is granted, the 3.20 p.m. ex Heybrook and the 4.0 p.m. ex Plymouth to be operated on weekdays only. Holiday arrangements :—Good Friday and Boxing Day, ordinary daily service (Winter schedule) except for first journey in either direction ; Bank Holidays, Saturday service (Summer schedule) ; Christmas Eve (Sundays excepted), service as on a Saturday (Winter schedule) ; Christmas Day, service suspended.

H.4899.—Messrs. **J. W. Newton and Sons** (Star Motor Service), of Downthomas, near Plymouth, between **Heybrook Bay** (Holiday Camp) and **Rack Corner**, via Downthomas and Langdon Lodge. The service to be operated daily from 1st June to 30th September and in conjunction with the service authorised under Application H.902. X.

					a.m.	a.m.	p.m.	p.m.	p.m.	p.m.	p.m.
Rack Corner	..	..	..	dep.	9.5	11.45	—	3.5	—	7.5	8.25
Downthomas	..	..	..	,,	9.7	—	1.47	—	5.47	—	8.27
Langdon Lodge	..	..	..	,,	—	11.47	—	3.7	—	7.7	—
Heybrook Bay (Holiday Camp)				arr.	9.14	11.53	1.54	3.13	5.54	7.13	8.34

					X.						
					a.m.	a.m.	p.m.	p.m.	p.m.	p.m.	p.m.
Heybrook Bay (Holiday Camp)				dep.	9.17	11.57	1.57	3.17	5.57	7.17	8.37
Langdon Lodge	..	..	..	,,	9.22	p.m.	2.2	—	6.2	7.22	8.42
Downthomas	..	..	..	,,	—	12.5	—	3.25	—	—	—
Rack Corner	..	..	..	arr.	9.25	12.7	2.5	2.5	—	6.5	7.25	8.45

X.—Not Sundays.

Holiday Camp.			
1d.	Spring Road (Cliff Road) Junction.		
2d.	1d.	Smock Park Lane.	
3d.	2d.	1d.	Langdon Lodge or Downthomas.
4d.	3d.	2d.	2d. Rack Corner.

To issue through bookings between this service and that authorised under the licence issued in respect of Application H.902.

Licence applications published in Western T.A. Notices & Proceedings 9th July 1934

J. W. Newton and Sons, of Down Thomas, near Plymouth, as follows :—

H.902.—**Heybrook Bay** and **Plymouth** (East Street), via Down Thomas, Langdon Court, Staddiscombe, Elburton and Billacombe. Modifications :—

(1) Summer :—To operate the 10.0 p.m. ex Down Thomas and the 10.35 p.m. ex Plymouth on Saturdays and Sundays only from June to August.

(2) To revise the Winter time tables, increasing the number of journeys :—

		N.S.	N.S.A.	N.S.			N.S.	N.S.A.			S.O.
		a.m.	a.m.	a.m.	p.m.	p.m.	p.m.	p.m.	p.m.	p.m.	p.m.
Heybrook Lodge	dep.	8.0	—	10.40	—	1.55	3.25	—	6.55	8.25	—
Down Thomas	,,	8.5	9.25	10.45	12.5	2.0	3.30	5.30	7.0	8.30	9.40
Staddiscombe	,,	8.10	9.30	10.50	12.10	2.5	3.35	5.35	7.5	8.35	9.45
Elburton	,,	8.15	9.35	10.55	12.15	2.10	3.40	5.40	7.10	8.40	9.50
Billacombe	,,	8.18	9.38	10.58	12.18	2.13	3.43	5.43	7.13	8.43	9.53
Plymouth	arr.	8.30	9.50	11.10	12.30	2.25	3.55	5.55	7.25	8.55	10.5

		N.S.		N.S.A.	N.S.			N.S.	N.S.A.			S.O.
		a.m.	a.m.	a.m.	a.m.	p.m.	p.m.	p.m.	p.m.	p.m.	p.m.	p.m.
Plymouth	dep.	8.40	10.0	11.20	12.40	2.40	4.10	6.10	7.40	9.10	10.10	
Billacombe	,,	8.52	10.12	11.32	12.52	2.52	4.22	6.22	7.52	9.22	10.22	
Elburton	,,	8.55	10.15	11.35	12.55	2.55	4.25	6.25	7.55	9.25	10.25	
Staddiscombe	,,	9.1	10.21	11.41	1.1	3.1	4.31	6.31	8.1	9.31	10.31	
Down Thomas	,,	9.6	10.26	11.46	1.6	3.6	4.36	6.36	8.6	9.36	10.36	
Heybrook Lodge	arr.	—	10.30	—	1.10	3.10	—	6.40	8.10	—	—	

N.S.—Not Sundays. N.S.A.—Not Sundays until April. S.O.—Saturdays only.

(3) Holiday arrangements :—To suspend the service on Christmas Day. Good Friday, Boxing Day and Easter Sunday—Sunday service as authorised for April. Easter Monday and Christmas Eve—Saturday Winter service. Other holidays—Summer Saturday service.

Application for revised services

N&P dated 2nd June 1936

EXPRESS CARRIAGE SERVICE.

H.6245.—**T. W. and A. W. Newton** (trading as J. W. Newton & Son), of Down Thomas, near Plymouth, between **Heybrook Bay** (Wembury Point Holiday Camp) and **Plymouth** (North Road Station), via Staddiscombe, Elburton, Billacombe and Plymouth. Route in Plymouth on the inward journey via Ebrington Street, Old Town Street and Cobourg Street ; and on the outward journey, via Cobourg Street, Tavistock Road and Ebrington Street.

To operate the service on Saturdays only, from Easter to the first Saturday in October (inclusive), in accordance with the following time schedule :—

		a.m.	p.m.	p.m. A
Heybrook Bay (Wembury Point Holiday Camp)	dep.	9.20	1.50	4.20
Plymouth (North Road Station)	arr.	9.55	2.25	4.55
Plymouth (North Road Station)	dep.	10.0	3.0	5.10
Heybrook Bay (Wembury Point Holiday Camp)	arr.	10.35	3.35	5.45

Fare, 1/- single.   A.—June to September only (inclusive).

Application for the Holiday Camp-Plymouth Station service

from N&P dated 16th May 1938

Chapter Three : The War Years

In September, 1939, J.W. Newton & Son was a thriving business running four 'buses, two taxis and two private cars. The 'buses were used on the regular daily service between Heybrook Bay and Plymouth, the holiday camp services and the school transport contract. Then, almost overnight with the outbreak of war, half the staff had gone, petrol was rationed, the holiday-makers were moving out and the troops were arriving to take over the camps. The holiday camp services were suspended for the duration of hostilities and Elsie Newton's sister, Ivy, returned home to help as a second conductress. More local girls were taken on, including Cis Labron (later Mrs Wright, post-mistress at Down Thomas, in which position she was succeeded by her daughter).

Men from the Ministry of War Transport arrived to tell Mr Newton that he could no longer purchase petrol from anyone he wished but had to buy 'pool' petrol. Headlights and interior lighting on the 'buses had to be masked and white paint applied to the edge of mudguards.

The blitz on Plymouth brought extreme difficulties for all 'bus operators and bombing raids inflicted heavy damage on the city of Plymouth. The buildings around the East Street terminus were flattened, roads blocked and temporary termini were used at Notte Street, Bruton Street (near Allen's Garage) and the Technical College (Pound Street) until the Star Motors returned to stand in East Street amid a scene of desolation. It was very confusing for the passengers who never knew from one day to the next where to find their 'bus.

During those dark days Newton's 'buses played an important role in getting people in and out of Plymouth where many were engaged on vital war work. At night they would be packed with people leaving the dangers of the city and the bombs. Bill Newton himself did not drive very much during the war being Chief Air Raid Warden for the district and also, for some time, a parish councillor.

Those times were recalled by Elsie Hudson (née Newton) in 1972:-

"Sitting here in the warmth of my sun-lounge, looking out on the garden and seeing the banners of Spring fluttering in the breeze, the daffodils, crocuses and almond blossom and the green grass making a lovely picture of all the good things in life; listening to the deep hum of a jumbo jet going over towards Heathrow Airport, carrying no doubt, a full load of passengers going about their various businesses, visiting from overseas or returning from distant travels, my thoughts wander back — is it really over thirty years ago — and I am in another time and another life it seems. Other aircraft, not so friendly, and other passengers: those we carried on our 'buses running to and from Plymouth and outlying country districts during the war and through the Plymouth blitz.

"There were times, although no one would admit it then, when we were all very frightened but you 'pressed on regardless' because everyone did just that and the spirit of togetherness was quite terrific. Everyone mattered to everyone else.

"The early part of the war had not brought much to test our endurance. In fact to a great number of us then, particularly the younger people, it had been in its way rather exciting. We had found ourselves in an entirely different world, a world of people in uniform. Servicemen everywhere, the A.R.P., the Home Guard. The black-out. And yet we still had the familiar things and places about us.

"I remember a small cafe in Westwell Street where I often had lunch with a couple of girl friends and a pub not far from there called the Picture Gallery, a fascinating place with its walls really covered with pictures of all kinds, sizes and subjects. One could still get a hot pasty from Sellecks for three-pence.

"Nearly everyone had a close relation in the forces. I had a brother with the British Expeditionary Force in France. A friend of mine had come home from Hong Kong, leaving her husband out there, and it still did not seem desperately serious.

"I was kept busy helping to keep my father's passenger transport business going. With that and the local A.R.P. (Air Raid Precaution) Warden Service I hadn't got time to stop and think of what might be ahead. But we were all to learn the hard way.

"A few small, scattered raids during the summer of 1940 brought a warning but still we were blessedly ignorant of what was to come. The first grim warning came on 28th November, 1940, when the oil tanks at Mount Batten were hit. In this raid ten people were killed at Oreston and a number of bombs fell around our home village of Down Thomas.

"I have a vivid memory of that night, coming out over Laira Bridge with our 'bus and the whole of the 'bank' looking out towards Mount Batten was covered with incendiary bombs. Can there be beauty in anything so dreadful? Was I quite without heart to be reminded of the lines "But oh! my friends and oh! my foes, was it a lovely light"?; really more like some grotesque fairyland.

"The raids continued spasmodically. My father was in the Prince of Wales Hospital, Greenbank, for a small operation on his arm when there was a raid one night. He discharged himself next morning, preferring to be up on his own feet and at home where he could keep in close touch with his business.

"The 'bus service continued without any major upheaval, having settled into a kind of routine after the chaos at the outbreak of war, until the evening of March 20th, 1941. We were standing at our terminus in East Street, waiting departure time, the 'bus almost full of passengers, when the air raid warning siren sounded. It was dark and then we could hear the drone of heavy aircraft approaching. It was not long before the first bombs started to fall and my driver, Ray Anderson, dashed across the road to the pub just next to Popham's Store. He called out to the servicemen going out on our 'bus. It was time to go now anyway, but by the time we were all aboard and started the pub roof was on fire, as was Selleck's Restaurant next door. Spooner's large store on the corner was ablaze and crumbling.

"We turned into Old Town Street without ever looking at the traffic lights. Were they working? The streets were suddenly empty of people and traffic anyway. Bombs were now dropping all around and fires raging everywhere. We came along Ebrington Street, it was just like daylight from the numerous fires and just past the Wesleyan Chapel there was a huge crater in the road, big enough to lose a 'bus in! So we turned up a side street to the left and a chimney stack crashed down inches in front of us. Up around behind Beaumont Park and a bomb screaming down landed with a thud just over the wall in the park. Our Guardian Angel must surely have been with us that night as it did not go off. I believe it exploded the next morning with devastating results. Up past Greenbank to Mutley Plain, looking for a way out of town.

"Eventually we got out somehow and found ourselves in a country road somewhere near Plympton. Here we stopped, for my driver to get out and walk a bit to reorientate his shaky legs and for us all to have a quick cigarette and to talk. We had all been unconsciously holding our breath and it was great to breathe somewhat freely again. We made the journey home and then we went back. You see we had other people relying on us to be there. We could not get right back into the centre, so it was a case of stopping where we could and getting out and going to look for our passengers."

'Plymouth Blitz -- The Story of the Raids' published by The Western Morning News notes:-
"This was easily the most terrifying raid that Plymouth had experienced. The Civil Defence organisations worked feverishly, but it was impossible to cope with the weight of the attack. They fought desperately all through the night against fearful odds and dangers.

"The dawn revealed the greatest tragedy in Plymouth's history. The scene of devastation was beyond description. Gaunt buildings, piles of smouldering rubble, miles of hose, the stench and the grime. Hollow-eyed for want of sleep, grimly silent, but still with an unconquerable spirit the people set about the task of clearing up .... The next night the attack was repeated on identical lines .... Altogether over 20,000 properties had been destroyed or badly damaged. The killed numbered 336."

Elsie Hudson continued:-
"Life became completely disorganized until the threads could again be gathered. Timetables went to pot but we got to and from Plymouth somehow. Another night we came out across Laira Bridge -- amazingly never hit -- and there were fires on both sides of the road to Plymstock Station. It was pretty hot, literally I thought our paint would blister. At the Plymstock Bridge there was a large crater in the road, so we had to make a detour again.

"Although one remembers some things so vividly, it can be difficult to recall things in their correct sequence. The pathetically sad sight of the continuous stream of people carrying their small children and a few precious belongings on the road out from Plymouth to anywhere in the surrounding countryside where they could find comparative safety for the night. One had seen pictures of this sort of thing happening in France but here in Plymouth it was unexpected and frightening. Yet people accepted it with a kind of dull resignation.

"We had many on our 'buses. 'Just take us out of town where it will be safe. We will sleep anywhere, under a hedge if needs be'. In the morning they would go back again, not knowing if they would find their homes still there.

"One morning a girl I knew got on the 'bus to go home, scruffy, dirty and tired out. She had been working for hours with a rescue team and all Gwen wanted to do was to sleep and forget it. Another girl, whose mother's bungalow had received a direct hit, came out on our 'bus to see what she could rescue. Fortunately mother had not been seriously hurt and I remember Dorothy standing there in tears looking at the smouldering ruin and wondering where to start.

"No one was a stranger in those days. Everyone helped everyone else in whatever way they could. We on the 'buses had inumerable requests. 'Will you get some pasties for me? No time for cooking today'. 'Will you take a message, deliver a package, get some shopping?' The funniest request I ever had was to buy a pair of corsets for a rather stout lady, which I reluctantly had to refuse, but wondered if she felt in need of some firm support.

"For the servicemen stationed out at Heybrook Bay we were a mobile fish and chip shop. We used to call at a little shop in Ebrington Street, where the people used to make up a special pack of fish and chips for our boys at sixpence a time. They would be picked up on the journey out of town and, packed around the engine, they kept hot until the end of the journey where the boys would be waiting for them.

"Our terminus in Plymouth was moved from place to place as one street after another became impassable. Most of our passengers found us or we found them. I don't think many got left behind. The last journey out at night created a bit of a problem. There was almost always a lot of passengers waiting, the biggest percentage being servicemen going the whole journey. We were not able to run extra 'buses because of petrol rationing and staff shortages, so we always tried to fill up with long distance passengers first. Those going no further than Elburton had the opportunity to catch other 'buses. We would carry as many as possible. After the thirty-two seater came in 1944 I can remember carrying over sixty at a time on this 'bus, mostly troops complete with gas masks and rifles. The friendly 'coppers' used to come round for a chat sometimes. We had names for most of them. There was 'Half-past-one' (Badge No.130), 'Sebastian' and 'Claude'. One of them told us that they liked seeing us around, we always had a cheerful smile. So I enlightened him by telling him 'that's done on purpose. While you are looking at our happy faces you haven't got time to count our standing passengers'.

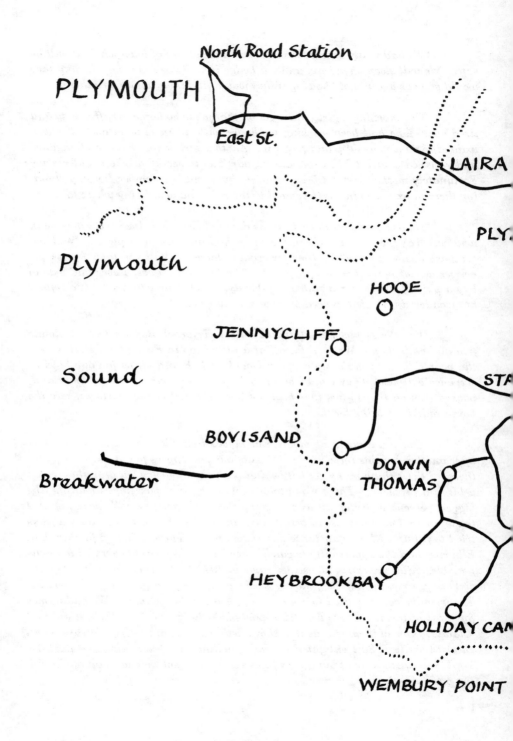

STAR MOTOR SERVICE *and*
HEYBROOK BAY MOTOR SERVICES

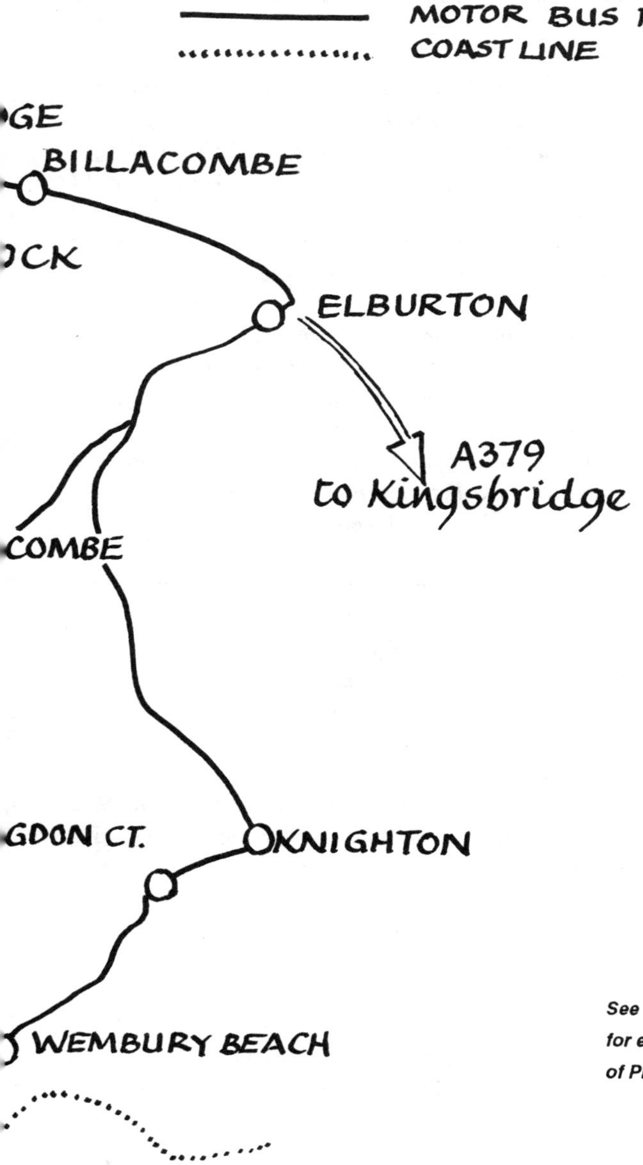

———————— MOTOR BUS ROUTES
..............., COAST LINE

GE

BILLACOMBE

)CK

ELBURTON

A379
to Kingsbridge

COMBE

GDON CT.   KNIGHTON

WEMBURY BEACH

See page 45
for enlargement
of Plymouth centre

"The last 'bus out on Saturday nights was nearly always a gay, lively occasion in spite of the tensions and circumstances. A Staff-Sergeant I knew from one of the camps used to bring me a pasty every Saturday and Jack and I would sit on the 'bus step — no room anywhere else — and I would eat it on the way home.

"My father was A.R.P. Warden for Down Thomas and district and this gave him plenty to do. He did not drive much himself, except when things were extra busy. Then he would turn out with the small 'bus - the 'Admiral's Barge', we called it! We would try to keep a steady pace on the road so that he could follow our rear lights. Driving in the black-out with masked headlights was not easy but he would give a toot-toot and pass us with a flourish. 'You can't hang around when Jerry's about', he would say, 'you've got to keep moving'.

"Three of our 'buses were commandeered on one occasion. We had to go to Kingsbridge Station and collect evacuee children from London and take them to the distribution centres in the outlying districts. These kids were marvellous. From tiny tots to twelve year olds, they were tired and hungry, with dirty, tear-stained faces. Yet still they managed a cheer when they saw the sea. 'Is that really the sea miss? I've never seen the sea before miss' Pathetic little mites they were then. I wonder how much of it all they still remember.

"It was a hectic life, sometimes sad, sometimes happy, but never quiet and peaceful. Poor old Plymouth was reduced to rubble and could never be the same again. We realised this but looking into the future was something we just did not do then. Coping with the present was enough in itself. Funnily enough the thing that scared me most was not one of the raids but a fight on the 'bus one night between three civilians. One very large man and his tiny wife versus another well-proportioned lady who was very well known in the city. They did not see eye to eye about a matter but there was not a policemen to be found that night. They were all far too busy with rescue work and firefighting services. We had a battle on our 'bus with brussels sprouts and beer bottles flying faster than enemy bombs. The relief when we got them off the 'bus was greater than hearing the 'all-clear' at the end of an air raid. My legs were quite wobbly for about the only time during the blitz.

"I must also mention the staff at the British Restaurant at the old Corn Exchange building. Those cheerful, efficient ladies we knew as Gladys, Pip and Melba always had a steaming 'cuppa' waiting for us whenever we had time for a break.

"*During the war when we carried a lot of servicemen, we normally had very little trouble. They were a pretty good bunch but on one occasion I had a couple of soldiers on the 'bus who were being rather difficult, using bad language and singing barrack-room songs! They were requested two or three times to stop but just carried on, so I warned them that if they continued any more they would be turned off the 'bus. They laughed and one of them, a heavy-weight type, said that I could not turn them off a public service vehicle.*

"*I asked him if he had ever read the regulations on the front of the timetable. When he asked what that had got to do with it, I quoted 'The proprietors reserve the right to refuse any bulky article likely to cause inconvenience' and reminded him that since it was a private firm and belonged to my family, I had the right to do just that. There was no further trouble.*

"*The blitz certainly took a lot from us but it gave a lot to us in comradeship and strength of purpose. Nevertheless I am glad my own children have been able to grow up in comparative peace. There is a world of difference between shadows of war and the real thing.*"

Star Motors Route 1 — **PLYMOUTH — HEYBROOK** — **89**

	WEEKDAYS									SUNDAY			
	a.m.	a.m.	a.m.	p.m.	p.m.	p.m.	p.m.	p.m.	p.m.	p.m.	p.m.	p.m.	p.m.
Plymouth	8 40	10 0	1120	1240	2 40	4 10	6 10	7 40	9 0	240	610	740	9 0
Billacombe	8 52	1012	1132	1252	2 52	4 22	6 22	7 52	9 12	252	622	752	912
Elburton	8 55	1015	1135	1255	2 55	4 25	6 25	7 55	9 15	255	625	755	915
Staddiscombe	9 1	1021	1141	1 1	3 1	4 31	6 31	8 1	9 21	3 1	631	8 1	921
Downthomas	9 6	1026	1146	1 6	3 6	4 36	6 36	8 6	9 26	3 6	636	8 6	926
Heybrook, Lodge ...	......	1030	......	1 53	3 10	......	6 40	8 10	......	310	640	810	.....

	WEEKDAYS									SUNDAY			
	a.m.	a.m.	a.m.	p.m.	p.m.	p.m.	p.m.	p.m.	p.m.	p.m.	p.m.	p.m.	p.m.
Heybrook, Lodge ...	8 0	......	1040	......	1 55	3 25	......	6 55	8 25	155	......	655	825
Downthomas	8 5	9 25	1045	12 5	2 0	3 30	5 30	7 0	8 30	2 0	530	7 0	830
Staddiscombe	8 10	9 30	1050	1210	2 5	3 35	5 35	7 5	8 35	2 5	535	7 5	835
Elburton	8 15	9 35	1055	1215	2 10	3 40	5 40	7 10	8 40	210	540	710	840
Billacombe	8 18	9 38	1058	1218	2 13	3 43	5 43	7 13	8 43	213	543	713	843
Plymouth	8 30	9 50	1110	1230	2 25	3 55	5 55	7 25	8 55	225	555	725	855

July 1943 timetable as published in Brendon's ABC Rail & Bus Guide
for Plymouth and Western Counties

TIME TABLE

Subject to Alteration at Short Notice

Heybrook Bay
Motor Services Ltd.

TO AND FROM

Plymouth, Elburton, Staddiscombe
Down Thomas and Heybrook Bay
(To Down Thomas for BOVISAND
and Langdon Court)
Terminus — East Street, Plymouth

PARCELS DELIVERED EN-ROUTE

Parcels forwarded in advance must be prepaid
to conductor

*The Proprietors reserve the right to refuse any
bulky article likely to cause inconvenience*

Although every effort will be made to keep to
the enclosed Schedule, no liability will be
accepted for failure to run at the stated times

Telephone : WEMBURY 227

HEYBROOK BAY MOTOR SERVICES LTD.

THE GARAGE, DOWN THOMAS, Nr. PLYMOUTH.   Wembury 227
H.902 SERVICE - Plymouth - Heybrook Bay - Wembury Point
Winter Service operating from 29th September, 1947 to   April 1948

	a.m.	a.m.	a.m.	noon	p.m	p.m	p.m	p.m	p.m	p.m	p.m	p.m
Heybrook Lodge ...	8.0	—	10.40	12.0	1.20	1.50	3.20	—	5.50	7.0	8.10	9.30
Wembury Point ...	—	9.15	—	—	—	—	—	4.36	—	—	—	—
Down Thomas	8.5	9.25	10.45	12.5	1.25	1.55	3.25	4.44	5.55	7.5	8.30	9.35
Staddiscombe	8.10	9.30	10.50	12.10	1.30	2.0	3.30	4.48	6.0	7.10	8.35	9.40
Elburton	8.15	9.35	10.55	12.15	1.35	2.5	3.35	4.53	6.5	7.15	8.40	9.45
Billacombe	8.20	9.40	11.0	12.20	1.40	2.10	3.40	4.58	6.10	7.20	8.45	9.50
Plymouth	8.30	9.50	11.10	12.30	1.50	2.20	3.50	5.8	6.20	7.30	8.55	10.0

Departures

	a.m.	a.m.	a.m.	p.m.	p.m	p.m	p.m	p.m	p.m	p.m	p.m	p.m
Plymouth	8.35	10.0	11.20	12.40	2.0	2.35	4.0	5.15	6.25	7.35	9.0	10.8
Billacombe	8.45	10.10	11.30	12.50	2.10	2.45	4.10	5.25	6.35	7.45	9.10	10.18
Elburton	8.50	10.15	11.35	12.55	2.15	2.50	4.15	5.30	6.40	7.50	9.15	10.23
Staddiscombe	8.55	10.20	11.40	1.0	2.20	2.55	4.20	5.35	6.45	7.55	9.20	10.28
Down Thomas	9.0	10.25	11.45	1.5	2.25	3.0	4.25	5.40	6.50	8.0	9.25	10.33
Wembury Point	9.8	—	—	—	—	—	4.34	—	—	—	—	—
Heybrook Lodge ...	—	10.30	11.50	1.10	2.30	3.5	—	5.45	6.55	8.5	9.28	—

* Not Sundays.   SUNDAY Service starts 9.25 Down Thomas then as printed with the
exception of Journeys Marked *.   Christmas Day No Service.
HIRES   May we quote for your next trip with our 32, 29, 24 or 20 Seaters day or evening hires
Book now for next Summer.   We give personal attention and guarantee complete satisfaction.

Timetable card issued for Winter 1947/8 service

Chapter Four : Heybrook Bay Motor Services

One day in 1943 Bill Newton met Mr Tom Hart, who in pre-war days had purchased an interest in the holiday camp at Wembury Point. The Hart family, who came from London, had some experience in the 'bus industry, having run the Enterprise Transport Co. Ltd. This was one of the many independent operators who had been taken over by the newly created London Passenger Transport Board during 1933/34. Five 'buses run on routes 14 and 26e had passed to the Board.

Bill Newton's health, always poor, had continued to worsen and in the course of conversation he mentioned that he was thinking of selling his 'bus business. Tom Hart saw that it could fit in well with his plans for the development of the holiday camp when it was returned to him after the war. He could see that private cars would be in short supply, that fuel would continue to be rationed but that people would want to travel again after the wartime restrictions. They would use the Star Motors service to reach the holiday camp. So negotiations commenced and these resulted in the sale of Bill Newton's 'bus services to Tom Hart in 1943.

As he was still serving in the armed forces Mr Hart was granted leave of absence to complete the transaction. A limited company with the title Heybrook Bay Motor Services Ltd was formed and this acquired the three buses then in service together with the Heybrook Bay - Plymouth service and the school contract work. Tom Hart subsequently returned to duty having arranged that Bill Newton would continue to run the business until he was demobilized.

Soon after, the Newton family suffered another tragedy when, early in 1944, the eldest son, Albert, who had been recalled to active service, died of wounds while serving with the Royal Engineers. The loss of a second son was another bitter blow.

With the war coming towards its end, the Ministry of War Transport was allowing a limited number of new 'buses to be delivered to operators in need. In April, 1944, Heybrook Bay Motor Services was allocated a Bedford with a utility standard body with seating for thirty-two passengers on wooden

29

slatted seats. The extra capacity was very useful and its arrival allowed the withdrawal from service of the oldest of the pre-war Bedfords which was eagerly snapped up for further service in Cornwall.

In 1945 Mr Hart returned from the war and Bill Newton was able to retire. His health had continued to deteriorate but this had not stopped him from working on the vehicles. On one occasion, after suffering a heart attack, he was found in the garage wielding a sledge-hammer in an effort to separate a tyre from a wheel. He also had an unusual method of checking spark-plugs, using his fingers and demonstrating how to make the sparks fly off the metal in his leg which was a legacy of his own army service.

In retirement he suffered a stroke, becoming first wheelchair-bound then confined to bed, but remained lovely and patient. He died, aged 60, on 1st January, 1949 and was buried in Wembury Churchyard on 5th January — his birthday. Over the years he had coped with considerable adversity, including his own disablement and the loss of two of his sons. In spite of this he built up a business which was well-known and well-loved in the district and which prided itself on personal service. In this he was ably supported by his wife, who brought up six children in the bungalow they built behind the garage at Down Thomas. This was no easy task as there were no modern conveniences. In due course the children also played a role in the business which was very much part of the day-to-day life of the villages to the east of Plymouth Sound and which was the way to the beach for so many Plymothians over the years.

The motor garage, car hire service and petrol sales at the Star Garage premises were retained by the Newton family after the sale of the 'bus services to Tom Hart. They passed to the two younger sons, John and Arthur, on their return from army service.

POST-WAR 'BUS SERVICES

On his demobilization in 1945 Tom Hart moved to Devon to take over the daily management of Heybrook Bay Motor Services Ltd with hopes that the holiday camp premises at Wembury Point would be returned to him. However, it soon became clear that the Royal Navy intended to retain the site for their gunnery school known as "H.M.S. Cambridge" and that it would not be returned. In view of this Mr Hart decided to develop the 'bus business.

With fuel still on ration and the supply of private cars restricted, the needs of the public who wanted to travel after the war-time restrictions had to be met by public transport. This was the situation which had been foreseen by

Mr Hart when he purchased the business. Therefore, private coach hire work was actively sought and the Heybrook Bay - Plymouth service continued with servicemen travelling, their presence making up for the lack of holidaymakers whom Mr Hart had hoped would be going to and from his holiday camp.

A new garage was built at the Plymouth end of Down Thomas village with fuel pumps for the supply of petrol to the general public. Mr and Mrs Hart then built a house for themselves behind the garage. Many of the familiar faces of the staff of Star Motors, including some of the Newton family, continued to serve the public as part of Heybrook Bay Motor Services.

At first the old East Street terminus in Plymouth continued in use but when New George Street was developed as part of the reconstruction of the blitzed city centre, the Heybrook Bay 'buses had to move, in 1953, to the improvised Buckwell Street Car Park at the top of Treville Street. Good loads were carried on the service, particularly during the morning and evening peak periods, and it remained the core of the business. However, some new opportunities arose.

Langdon Court is a large house situated between Down Thomas and Wembury. It was converted for use as a convalescent home and patients could have visitors on Sunday afternoons between 2 p.m. and 4 p.m. To cater for their needs, Heybrook Bay Motor Services introduced an express service which left Plymouth at 1.30 p.m. and returned from the home at 4.10 p.m. Fares were one shilling single, one shilling and eightpence return. This service ran for some four and a half years until the number of passengers fell, the special journeys were withdrawn and the normal service 'bus to Heybrook Bay was diverted to call at Langdon Court.

A further opportunity arose as the result of road improvements which enabled 'buses to run down to Bovisand Bay from Staddiscombe. In the summer of 1952 a licence was obtained to run eight journeys a day between Plymouth and Bovisand at peak traffic times. No longer was it necessary for Tom Hart with his binoculars to stand at the top of the track leading up from Bovisand to Down Thomas trying to count the numbers making their way up to the 'bus. This was especially necessary if the weather had worsened suddenly and the motor boats which ferried passengers across from the Barbican could not come back to take them home. Then they joined the considerable numbers who had come by 'bus. As traffic developed duplicates were run, some direct via Exeter Street (instead of Ebrington Street) to Bovisand without picking up en route. When traffic was quiet a shuttle service would be run to and from

Bovisand, connecting with the Plymouth - Heybrook Bay service at Staddiscombe.

As has been mentioned previously, sailors from H.M.S. Cambridge travelled to and from Plymouth on the 'buses and by 1947 two journeys a day had been diverted to serve the establishment. One arrived from Plymouth just after 9 a.m., the other left for the city just after 4.30 p.m. As traffic grew so the number of journeys to and from the camp increased until seven outward and return journeys ran via Wembury Point. This movement of service personnel certainly helped to sustain the Plymouth service during the times when private car ownership increased and the number of 'bus passengers nationally diminished.

School contract work on behalf of Devon County Council also grew. The Plymstock - Down Thomas and Wembury route, inherited from Bill Newton, continued and during 1948 two more daily runs were obtained. The first of these was for the conveyance of younger children from the Heybrook Bay area to and from Hooe Primary School. The vehicle on this contract was not allowed to use the coast road at Jennycliff when carrying passengers as it was considered too dangerous. Also, from the autumn of that year, a 32-seater was provided to carry Grammar School pupils living in the Wembury area to and from Plympton. From 1957 Heybrook Bay Motor Services also ran a 29-seater coach between Plympton Grammar School and Ermington to take an overload which could not be accommodated on the main contract vehicles.

In March, 1958 the new Bretonside Bus Station was opened in Plymouth and the Heybrook Bay - Plymouth service terminus was transferred there. Heybrook Bay Motor Services vehicles now stood among numbers of Western National and Plymouth Corporation vehicles, being the only independent operators service to run into the city daily.

PRINCESS TOURS

With private coach hire work expanding in the post-war years, Mr Hart could see that there was tremendous potential for business from the city of Plymouth, which had nearly a quarter of a million population. Rather than start from scratch he looked for an opportunity to purchase an existing business.

Fred Coombes kept a shop in Station Road, Keyham, and during the 1920's ran the "Rosebud", a fourteen seater char-a-banc. He also acquired the coach business of a local coalman by the name of Thorn and by 1930 had

CDR 940 on a well loaded service journey on 3rd August, 1952. (A.B. Cross)

The Bedford OB model was a popular choice for independent 'bus and coach operators in post World War Two years. The first of the type to be bought by Heybrook Bay Motor Services Ltd was DCO 99, which had coach seats. It is seen here with Mrs Ivy Bone (née Newton) and her two children, Jenny and John, in front.

Elsie Newton obtained her Conductor's badge in March, 1939, at the age of twenty-two. She is seen holding a rack of tickets and is wearing her ticket punch and a leather cash bag.

In 1955, Mr Hart bought two Commer Avenger coaches for his fleet. The fuel economy of these vehicles was excellent but they could be very noisy. KJY 205 is pictured above. (East Pennine Transport Group - R.Marshall collection)

A most unusual purchase was this second-hand Tilling-Stevens with a Meadows engine. Together with the Commers it was used on private-hire and forces leave services. (East Pennine Transport Group - R. Marshall collection)

FCO 111 was another OB model Bedford but this had 'bus type seats. It was purchased in August 1949 and is seen here on 30th July, 1952, in a cream and red livery on one of the new roundabouts which were part of the reconstructed centre of Plymouth. (A.B. Cross)

A Heybrook Bay Motor Services vehicle passes through Elburton on a service journey. It is probably FCO 111 in the maroon, red and cream livery.

Pictured at Bretonside Bus Station, the driver of Bedford OB EDR 345 wears a traditional peaked cap with white cover and, from the badge on the radiator, appears to be a member of the Bedford Drivers Club. (East Pennine Transport Group - R. Marshall collection)

A second Bedford SB was purchased in July, 1951. This was MOD 688 seen here on route to Heybrook Bay on 3rd August, 1952. (A.B. Cross)

This 40-seater Bedford was bought by Heybrook Bay Motor Services in 1954 to work the local bus services. RTA 97 is seen at Bretonside Bus Station loading for a trip to Wembury Point. (East Pennine Transport Group - R. Marshall collection)

The last vehicle to be purchased by Heybrook Bay Motor Services Ltd was this Bedford with a 40-seat body by Duple Midland. It was one of two Heybrook Bay vehicles previously operated by Scottish operator Hutchison of Overtown and is seen at Plymouth Bretonside Bus Station awaiting departure for Wembury Point. Two very relaxed potential passengers appear to be playing "book-ends".

adopted the fleetname "Princess Tours". Up to two vehicles were run on excursions and tours from the city and private hire work was also undertaken.

Following the death of Mr Coombes in the 'thirties, his wife ran the business until the war caused operations to be suspended. In 1947 Mrs S. Coombes took up the licence to run excursions and tours again and in due course sought a buyer. Mr Hart formed a new company, Coombes (Plymouth) Ltd, which traded as Princess Tours, to take over the licences, thus establishing a base in the city.

Business was commenced with a second-hand Bedford 29-seater coach and a licence to use one vehicle on tours, with a second on Bank Holidays. Two new Bedfords were acquired in due course and these joined the original coach. By 1952 an office had been opened at 1, Tavistock Road, Drake Circus, in the centre of Plymouth. The premises were shared with a firm of coal merchants, Hooper, Martin & Truscott. Bookings were taken for excursions and tours and for private coach hire but through the Princess Tours business, party organisers were offered more than just coach hire. Tickets could be obtained for shows and sporting events, hotels could be booked and meals arranged en route.

Princess Tours continued as a separate legal entity but worked very closely with Heybrook Bay Motor Services, a joint publicity booklet being produced. This gave suggestions for party organisers as well as details of the Heybrook Bay 'bus services. From 1954, only two vehicles were licensed in the name of Coombes (Plymouth) Ltd. but operations continued in the name of Princess Tours, the city centre office moving to Bretonside Bus Station when it opened in March, 1958. The office on the concourse was adjacent to the terminus of the Heybrook Bay 'bus service.

LEAVE SERVICES

A major factor in the life of many young men after the Second World War was the requirement that they undertook two years in the armed services. This conscription was known as 'National Service'. The consequence was that many young men were posted to various parts of the world to become sailors, soldiers or airmen. Being away from home, especially family, wives or girl friends, was not something that many of them enjoyed and for those serving in U.K. bases their aim was to get home as often as leave passes and finances allowed.

Devonport Naval Base had a large number of National Servicemen and they had regular long or short weekend leave passes. Train services were often not convenient so, in the early 1950's, they started getting together and hiring coaches in which to travel home for the weekend. The main coach operator involved in this work was Blakes (Continental) Tours Ltd of Plymouth. As runs became regular they gained licences to run express services from the Royal Naval Barracks at Devonport. From March, 1951 they ran to Birmingham, Portsmouth and London, later adding Liverpool, Sheffield, Penzance and Swansea.

As traffic grew, Blakes hired in other operators to help, among them Heybrook Bay Motor Services. Tom Hart then decided that he, too, would seek licences so in February, 1952 he applied to run to Manchester and Liverpool. This application was unsuccessful but, undaunted, fresh attempts were made to obtain some of the traffic from Wembury Point and Devonport to Birmingham, Liverpool, Manchester, Portsmouth and London. Western National also applied for similar services. After hearing the evidence the Traffic Commissioners decided that the three operators should share the traffic and granted Heybrook Bay Motor Services licences for routes to Birmingham, Liverpool and Portsmouth. From January, 1953, there was a rota system which ensured each operator took their turn. This was as follows:-

Birmingham Service
Operator:
1. Blakes
2. Heybrook Bay
3. Blakes
4. Heybrook Bay

Liverpool Service
Operator:
1. Blakes
2. Blakes
3. Heybrook Bay
4. Western National
5. Blakes

Portsmouth Service
Operator:
1. Blakes
2. Blakes
3. Western National
4. Heybrook Bay
5. Blakes
6. Western National
7. Heybrook Bay
8. Blakes
9. Western National
10. Western National
11. Western National

The strength of the desire to get home for the weekend is shown by the schedule for the Liverpool service. The coach left Devonport at 4.30 p.m. on Friday afternoon, taking 16 hours to reach its destination in those pre-motorway days when the A38 between Plymouth and Bristol was described as the longest lane in England. There would then be 18 hours to enjoy at home before setting out again at 3 p.m. on Sunday for another 16 hour journey back, arriving at the Barracks at 7 a.m. on Monday morning in time to start a day's work. Journey times were calculated at an average speed of 15 miles per hour in built up areas and 20 m.p.h. in rural areas. The return fare was £2.7s.3d. From 1953 an increase in the scheduled speed to an overall 22 m.p.h. was allowed and this cut the scheduled journey time to Liverpool by an hour and twenty minutes. For servicemen on short weekend passes, additional journeys left the Devonport Barracks at midday on Saturdays, again returning for the 7 a.m. start on Monday morning.

If the leave services were to be profitable it was necessary to find work for the vehicles on Saturdays, rather than leave them standing idle at their destinations. Arrangements were made to hire the coaches to other operators and they would work excursions and private-party outings or duplicate journeys for Royal Blue Express Services and Associated Motorways.

The volume of traffic was such that the amount of administration was considerable. In 1955, with Blakes under some pressure, it was decided that in future Heybrook Bay Motor Services, Western National and Blakes would each have a one-third share in the operation of all the leave services from the port. Western National undertook the bookings and ticket issue and three members of their staff would go to the Naval Barracks each Friday afternoon and Saturday morning. A trestle table and chairs would be set up with a book of tickets and cash tin at hand. At a given signal the doors would open and in would surge several hundred eager matelots, cash in hand, shouting their destinations and wanting immediate attention. Their aim was to get mobile as soon as possible. In the melée it was essential not to let go of the ticket until one had a firm grip on the money, otherwise it was not unknown for the cash, ticket and sailor to disappear back into the crowd, leaving the unfortunate booking clerk to make up the shortage on his return to depot.

There was also the problem that occasionally there might be some unauthorised passengers on the return journey, usually a sailor returning from extended leave who had evaded the drivers check. Western National charged one young trainee with the task of standing on the Exeter By-Pass at 4 a.m. on Monday mornings in order to check the tickets on returning leave service coaches. To wake up a coach load of sleeping sailors, all depressed at having to leave home for another week in Barracks, and ask to see their tickets could be a memorable experience! Tripping over the body of a sleeping Able-Bodied Seaman stretched out along the aisle provoked a response that was unprintable. It could be a dangerous way to make a living.

Basil Williams, the principal shareholder in Blakes (Continental) Tours, was also Managing Director of Hants & Sussex Motor Services Ltd but the latter ceased trading late in 1954.   There had been a reliance on the Plymouth vehicles inter-working with Hants & Sussex and without this Blakes found the leave services unremunerative.   They struggled on during 1955 but the company went into receivership in January 1956.   The fleet was gradually run down as Blakes withdrew from operation of the leave services in the spring of 1956 and Haybrook Bay and Western National now shared the traffic equally between them.   Blakes continued to run excursions until the autumn when the tours licences were acquired by the Embankment Motor Co. (Plymouth) Ltd and the last vehicles were disposed of.

VEHICLES

The growth in the business in post-war years was rapid and is well illustrated by looking at the size of the fleet.   When Mr Hart returned from the war in 1945 there were four 'buses.   Within three years the fleet had doubled and by 1951, with the acquisition of Princess Tours, the combined fleet of Heybrook Bay Motor Services and Coombes (Plymouth) Ltd numbered thirteen 'buses and coaches.   It remained thus until the middle of the decade when Blakes (Continental) Tours ceased operations and Heybrook Bay and Western National shared the forces leave traffic between them.   This called for extra vehicles and so numbers increased to seventeen in 1957.

In the early post-war years a livery of maroon, red and cream was adopted but with a newer shape of vehicle coming into service this was altered to an attractive red and cream during the 1950's.   Bedford remained the favourite make and petrol engines were usual.   However, as coaches undertook longer journeys on the forces leave services and also some relief work for the Royal Blue Express Services of the Western and Southern National, diesel engined vehicles were bought.   Generally purchases were of new vehicles but occasionally a good, second-hand model joined the fleet.

Some other makes were also tried.   A Leyland, intended for a London operator but never delivered to them, was the first non-Bedford to enter the Heybrook Bay fleet.   1955 saw the purchase of a second-hand Tilling-Stevens, the only vehicle of that make to see service with the company.   It is remembered for the necessity to use a starting handle to bring it into life.   This needed considerable care if a 'kick-back' was to be avoided and one driver received a very nasty blow to the face as the handle shot back round as the engine roared into life.   During 1955-56 three Commers were bought for use on the forces leave services.   These were thrifty but throaty; they returned excellent fuel consumption figures but are remembered for the unmistakable exhaust notes and, it must be said, for some initial unreliability.

36

CONCLUSION

Although Mr Hart had not been able to secure the return of the holiday camp premises at Wembury Point after the war, he still had ambitions in the holiday business. Thus, when the Bovisand Lodge Estate came on to the market during the late 1950's, he purchased it. It was hoped to utilize Heybrook Bay Motor Services staff during the winter months for, although the coach business was seasonal, no one was laid off during the quiet periods.

Within a short time of the purchase being completed Mr Tom Hart suffered a heart attack. He remained ill for some time and his doctor strongly advised that he should reduce his business interests, so the decision was made to sell Heybrook Bay Motor Services and to retain the Bovisand Lodge Estate.

With Mr Hart very ill, it was left to Mrs Peggy Hart to enter into negotiations with Western National. Agreement was reached to transfer all operations including the local 'bus services between Plymouth, Wembury Point, Heybrook Bay and Bovisand as well as the share in the forces leave services, the Princess Tours excursions and the private hire work. One vehicle was to pass to Western National, the rest were to be disposed of by Mr and Mrs Hart and it was agreed that the new owners would take over with effect from 1st January, 1959. From that morning the last regular daily, independent 'bus service into Plymouth passed to its new owners, becoming Plymouth Joint Services routes 54 and 55. Regrettably Mr Hart died but his widow, Peggy, and his son, John, have continued in business and in public life in the area.

Many Plymothians fondly remember the days of Newton's Star Motors and Hart's Heybrook Bay Motor Services. Between them they served the travelling public for some thirty-five years, providing a personal, friendly and reliable service at a time when the motor-bus was an essential part of daily life.

Gone but not forgotten.

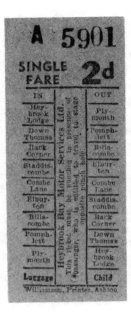

Examples of tickets used and of the
self-advertisement on the reverse
of some of them (actual size)

THE PEOPLE

Star Motor Service -- Newton family and known staff

James William (Bill) Newton   Proprietor
Mrs Bertha Newton   ...   wife of J.W. Newton
and their children:-

Albert ...	...	Partner; worked in business 1937 - 1939
Harold ...	...	Partner
Elsie ...	...	Secretary; later Conductress
Ivy ...	...	Conductress, early war years
Arthur ...	...	Garage hand, 1940-1945
John ...	...	Ran Star Garage, Down Thomas in post war

years, some time with Arthur, then on own account.

Harry Bone	... ...	Ivy's husband - Conductor/Driver 1939
Ernie Harwood ...	...	Driver
Jack Ash	... ...	Conductor
Fred Toms	... ...	Driver
Harold Hobbs	... ...	Conductor
Bill Saunders	... ...	Driver
Mark Farnell	... ...	Mechanic
Bill Kemp	... ...	Driver
Gordon Blagdon ...	...	Conductor
Lloyd Lapthorn ...	...	Garage hand; Conductor
Ray Anderson	... ...	Driver
Geoff Williams	... ...	Driver
Cis Labron	... ...	Conductress
Myrtle Lamb	... ...	Conductress
Vera Labron	... ...	Conductress
Bob Lidstone	... ...	Driver
Sid Raynor	... ...	Driver
Reg Wordsworth ...	...	Driver

BUS SERVICE

HEYBROOK BAY MOTOR SERVICES LTD., THE GARAGE, DOWN THOMAS, Near PLYMOUTH.   Telephone WEMBURY 227

Daily Service operating from second Monday in September to last Monday in July, excluding Saturdays and Sundays, May—Sept. inclusive, when full summer service operates :

H.902 Service.   Plymouth — HEYBROOK BAY — WEMBURY POINT — BOVISAND

	†	†	†	Sun. only	Sun. only	†	†	Sat. only	†	† TSO	Sun. only	†						†		Sun. only
	a.m.	a.m.	a.m.	a.m.	a.m.	a.m.	a.m.	p.m.	p.m.	p.m.	p.m.	p.m.	p.m.	p.m.	p.m.	p.m.	p.m.	p.m.	p.m.	p.m.
HEYBROOK BAY	7.00	8.00	....	....	10.45	10.40	12.00	....	1.05	....	1.50	3.20	....	4.35	....	5.50	....	8.05	9.50	9.50
WEMBURY POINT	....	7.53	9.15	....	10.40	....	....	12.00	....	1.13	....	....	4.35	....	6.58	....	....	....		
DOWN THOMAS	7.04	8.05	9.25	9.25	10.50	10.45	12.05	....	1.25	....	1.55	3.25	4.44	5.55	7.05	8.45	10.10	10.00		
STADDISCOMBE	7.08	8.10	9.30	9.30	10.55	10.50	12.10	....	1.30	....	2.00	3.30	4.48	6.00	7.10	8.50	10.15	10.05		
ELBURTON	7.15	8.15	9.35	9.35	11.00	10.55	12.15	....	1.35	....	2.05	3.35	4.53	6.05	7.15	8.55	10.20	10.10		
BILLACOMBE	7.18	8.20	9.40	9.40	11.05	11.00	12.20	....	1.40	....	2.10	3.40	4.58	6.10	7.20	9.00	10.25	10.15		
PLYMOUTH	7.28	8.30	9.50	9.50	11.15	11.10	12.30	....	1.50	....	2.20	3.50	5.08	6.20	7.30	9.10	10.35	10.25		

	†	†	†	†˟	Sun. only	Sun. only	†	† TSO	†	Sun. only								†		Sun. only
	a.m.	a.m.	a.m.	a.m.	a.m.	a.m.	p.m.	p.m.	p.m.	p.m.	p.m.	p.m.	p.m.	p m.	p.m.	p.m.	p.m.	p.m.		p.m.
PLYMOUTH	7.30	8.35	10.00	10.00	11.20	11.20	12.35	....	2.00	....	2.35	4.00	5.15	6.25	7.35	9.15	10.45	10.30		
BILLACOMBE	7.40	8.45	10.10	10.10	11.30	11.30	12.45	....	2.10	....	2.45	4.10	5.25	6.35	7.45	9.25	10.55	10.40		
ELBURTON	7.45	8.50	10.15	10.15	11.35	11.35	12.50	....	2.15	....	2.50	4.15	5.30	6.40	7.50	9.30	11.00	10.45		
STADDISCOMBE	7.50	8.55	10.20	10.20	11.40	11.40	12.55	....	2.20	....	2.55	4.20	5.35	6.45	7.55	9.35	11.05	10.50		
LANGDON COURT								1.13		3.00*						9.38	11.08	10.53		
DOWN THOMAS	7.55	9.00	10.25	10.25	11.45	11.45	1.00	....	2.25	....	3.02	4.25	5.40	6.50	8.00	9.45	11.18	11.05		
WEMBURY POINT	7.53	9.08	....	10.30	....	....	....	1.13	....	....	....	4.33	....	6.58			11.13	11.00		
HEYBROOK BAY	7.58	....	10.30	10.45	11.50	11.50	1.05	....	2.30	....	3.05	....	5.45	....	8.05	9.50	11.22	11.10		

† Not Sundays.   Service starts 9.25 a.m., Down Thomas.
TSO.   Thursdays and Saturdays only.
Sun. only.   Sunday only.

Sat. only.   Saturdays only.
* 3 p.m. Langdon Court. Sunday only.
Christmas Day : No service. Bank Holidays as Sundays.

BOVISAND.   Tuesdays and Fridays only

BOVISAND depart ... 9.15 a.m.	STADDISCOMBE depart ... 1.00 p.m.
STADDISCOMBE arrive ... 9.23 a.m.	BOVISAND arrive ... 1.08 p.m.

PLYMOUTH TERMINUS. Buckwell Street Car Park.   Top of Treville Street.

FIRST MONDAY IN JUNE—LAST MONDAY IN JULY THE ABOVE BOVISAND SERVICE DAILY

*1.50 p.m. ex Heybrook Bay | operates first Monday in June to
*2.35 p.m. ex Plymouth | second Monday in September.

This and the following two pages reproduce the Heybrook Bay Summer Timetable
including suggestions for tour organisers and a map of the Plymouth terminus

SUMMER SERVICE

HEYBROOK BAY MOTOR SERVICES LTD., THE GARAGE, DOWN THOMAS, Near PLYMOUTH.   Telephone WEMBURY 227

Daily Summer Service operating from last Monday in July until second Monday in September, and week-ends, Saturdays, and Sundays, from May to September inclusive.

H.902 Service.   Plymouth — HEYBROOK BAY — WEMBURY POINT — BOVISAND

	† a.m.	† a.m.	† a.m.	a.m.	Sun. only a.m.	a.m.	a.m.	a.m.	p.m.	p.m.	p.m.	p.m.	p.m.	p.m.	p.m.	p.m.	p.m.	p.m.	p.m.	† p.m.	Sun. only p.m.
HEYBROOK BAY	7.00	8.00		10.00	10.45	10.40	11.20	12.00	1.05	1.50	2.40	3.20	4.40	5.50	7.00	7.55	8.05	9.50	9.50		
WEMBURY POINT		7.53	9.15		10.40			12.00‡	1.13			4.08 ·	5.20	6.35							
DOWN THOMAS	7.04	8.05	9.25	10.05	10.50	10.45	11.25	12.05	1.25	1.55	2.45	3.25	4.15	4.44	5.25	5.55	6.40	7.05	8.00	8.45	10.10	10.00
STADDISCOMBE	7.08	8.10	9.30	10.10	10.55	10.50	11.30	12.10	1.30	2.00	2.50	3.30	4.20	4.48	5.30	6.00	6.45	7.10	8.05	8.50	10.15	10.05
ELBURTON	7.15	8.15	9.35	10.15	11.00	10.55	11.35	12.15	1.35	2.05	2.55	3.35	4.25	4.53	5.35	6.05	6.50	7.15	8.10	8.55	10.20	10.10
BILLACOMBE	7.18	8.20	9.40	10.20	11.05	11.00	11.40	12.20	1.40	2.10	3.00	3.40	4.30	4.58	5.40	6.10	6.55	7.20	8.15	9.00	10.25	10.15
PLYMOUTH	7.28	8.30	9.50	10.30	11.15	11.10	11.50	12.30	1.50	2.20	3.10	3.50	4.40	5.08	5.50	6.20	7.05	7.30	8.25	9.10	10.35	10.25

	† a.m.	† a.m.	† a.m.	a.m.	Sun. only a.m.	a.m.	a.m.	p.m.	p.m.	p.m.	p.m.	p.m.	p.m.	p.m.	p.m.	p.m.	p.m.	p.m.	p.m.	† p.m.	Sun. only p.m.
PLYMOUTH	7.30	8.35	10.00	10.10	10.40	11.20	12.00	12.35	2.00	2.35	3.20	4.00	4.45	5.15	6.00	6.25	7.15	7.35	8.30	9.15	10.45	10.45
BILLACOMBE	7.40	8.45	10.10	10.10	10.50	11.30	12.10	12.45	2.10	2.45	3.30	4.10	4.55	5.25	6.10	6.35	7.25	7.45	8.40	9.25	10.55	10.40
ELBURTON	7.45	8.50	10.15	10.15	10.55	11.35	12.15	12.50	2.15	2.50	3.35	4.15	5.00	5.30	6.15	6.40	7.30	7.50	8.45	9.30	11.00	10.45
STADDISCOMBE	7.50	8.55	10.20	10.20	11.00	11.40	12.20	12.55	2.20	2.55	3.40	4.20	5.05	5.35	6.20	6.45	7.35	7.55	8.50	9.35	11.05	10.50
LANGDON COURT									2.23*											9.38	11.08	10.53
DOWN THOMAS	7.55	9.00	10.25	10.25	11.05	11.45	12.25	1.00	2.25	3.00	3.45	4.25	5.10	5.40	6.25	6.50	7.40	8.00	8.55	9.45	11.18	11.05
WEMBURY POINT	7.53	9.08		10.30				1.13		3.53		5.15		6.30							11.13	11.00
HEYBROOK BAY	7.58	...	10.30	10.45	11.10	11.50	12.30	1.05	2.30	3.05		4.30		5.45		6.55	7.45	8.05		9.50	11.22	11.10

SUNDAY SERVICE STARTS 9.25 a.m. Down Thomas

† Not Sundays.   ‡ Saturdays only.   SUN. ONLY. Sundays only.   * 2 p.m. Langdon Court Sundays only.   Bank Holidays as Sundays.

BOVISAND EXTENSION (coincident with running times set out above)

	a.m.	a.m.	a.m.	p.m.	p.m.	p.m.	p.m.	p.m.
STADDISCOMBE dept.	10.20	11.00	11.40	2.20	2.55	6.20	6.50	7.35
BOVISAND arr.	10.28	11.08	11.48	2.28	3.03	6.28	6.58	7.43
BOVISAND dept.	10.40	11.20	11.50	2.40	5.50	6.35	7.00	7.55
STADDISCOMBE arr.	10.48	11.28	11.58	2.48	5.58	6.43	7.08	8.03

Coaches for hire 26, 29, 33 or 41 seaters.   May we quote you?   Telephone Wembury 227.   Summer Service MAY week-ends only. Full Daily Summer Service starts last Monday in July.

PLYMOUTH TERMINUS.   Buckwell Street Car Park.   Top of Treville Street

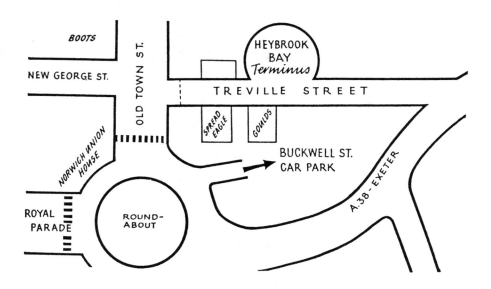

HOLIDAY TOURS

Seven, eight, ten, fourteen days or as required. Why not suggest this way of having the annual holiday to your party?

We can arrange to quote you inclusive prices, covering road travel charge, all meals and hotel accommodation—everything arranged. Suggestions gladly forwarded. Wales, Blackpool and the Lake District, Scotland, East Coast, London, etc.,—delightful "all-in" tours can be planned. The really ideal holiday—relaxing and carefree. Worth thinking over!

Introduction

Here are a variety of attractive suggestions for day and half-day tours, covering Devon, Cornwall, Somerset and Dorset. We shall be most pleased to quote you for any you may think suitable for your Party, or for any other routes you yourself may devise.

Addresses for meals can be supplied, or taken from Advertisers enclosed or if you prefer it so, we will arrange for you. Hotels can be booked if required, every co-operation is yours. Our aim is to help in all travel problems personally, and to make each Tour a thoroughly enjoyable and satisfactory one; something always to be remembered.

Coaches are really Luxurious and Radio Equipped. 41, 36, 33, 29 and 26 Seater Coaches are available.

May we look forward to receiving your enquiry? Our personal attention is sincerely at your service and care-free travel is *Yours*.

To: ORGANISERS OF STAFF, FAMILY, CLUBS, GUILD OR CHURCH OUTINGS this BOOKLET is intended for you!

Yours faithfully,

HEYBROOK BAY MOTORS SERVICES LTD.

Wembury 227

THE VEHICLES

Seating code: B = Bus, C = coach followed by number of seats.

J.W. Newton & Son — Fleet List 1922-1943
Fleet name: Star Motor Service (known locally as "Red Star")

Regn.No.	Make/Model	Body	Seats	New	Acquired	Sold
TA 1853	Ford 22.4hp	?	B14	1921	Dec.1922	Sep.1925
TA 5643	Ford 'A'	Hendra	B14	1923	ca. 1925	Jun.1926
TT 7840	Morris	?	B14	1926	ca. 1926	1931
DR 7888	Chevrolet U	Mumford	B14	1930	Jan.1931	1935
DR 9379	Bedford WLB	Mumford	B20	1931	Nov.1931	1937
KP 9701	Chevrolet LQ	Waveney	B14	1929	Jun.1935	ca. 1943
JY 6332	Bedford WLB	Duple	B20	1935	Aug.1935	Oct.1943
JY 9486	Bedford WTB	?	B20	1937	Jan.1937	Oct.1943
BCO 510	Bedford WTB	Waveney	B24	1938	Aug.1938	Oct.1943

Notes:
Unless otherwise stated below, vehicles were purchased new.
TA 1853 was originally a char-a-banc of Burgess, Bradninch. The chassis was sold to Waterfall, Looe in September, 1921 but the body was retained by Burgess. Change of owner in December, 1922 to unknown owner, Plymouth (? dealer) from whom Mr. Newton purchased it.
TA 5643 was previously operated by Hendra (Totnesia Cars), Totnes.
TT 7840 was new to Joshua Boyd, Links Hotel, Thurlestone in April, 1926.
KP 9701 was previously with Maidstone & District Motor Services (No. 823). They had acquired it from Tunbridge Wells Victor Transport Co. Ltd. in May, 1935.
JY 9486 may have had a Waveney body.
BCO 510 has been reported as having a body by Mulliner but Newton's records clearly show it as being bodied by Waveney.

JY 6332, JY 9486 and BCO 510 passed to Heybrook Bay Motor Services Ltd on the formation of that company following the purchase of the business of Star Motor Service by Mr Tom Hart.

LIVERY:
Blue up to waistrail, red above with white roof and lettering and gold star emblem. (TA 1853 and TA 5643 shown in motor taxation records as Blue)

Heybrook Bay Motor Services Ltd — Fleet List 1943-1959

Regn.No.	Make/Model	Body	Seats	New	Acquired	Sold
JY 6332	Bedford WLB	Duple	B20	1935	Oct.1943	Aug.1944
JY 9486	Bedford WTB	?	B20	1937	Oct.1943	Sep.1951
BCO 510	Bedford WTB	Waveney	B24	1938	Oct.1943	May 1951
CDR 780	Bedford OWB	Duple	B32	1944	Apl.1944	May 1952
CDR 940	Bedford OWB	Duple	B32	1945	Oct.1945	Jul.1954
DCO 99	Bedford OB	Duple	C29	1946	May 1946	Feb.1954
OMY 837	Bedford OB	Pearson	B26	1947	Nov.1947	Feb.1954
KTA 17	Bedford OB	Duple	C29	1948	Sep.1948	Jan.1959
EDR 345	Bedford OB	Duple	C29	1948	Nov.1948	Jan.1959
FCO 111	Bedford OB	Mulliner	B28	1949	Aug.1949	Jan.1959
MTA 917	Bedford OB	Duple	C29	1951	Jan.1951	Jan.1959
MOD 541	Bedford SB	Duple	C33	1951	Jul.1951	Jan.1959
MOD 688	Bedford SB	Brush	C33	1951	Jul.1951	May 1956
XMT 624	Leyland PSU1	Burlingham	C41	1952	Jun.1952	Jan.1959
FHS 486	Bedford SB	Duple	C33	1952	Mar.1954	Jan.1959
PDV 557	Bedford SB	Duple	C36	1954	Mar.1954	Jan.1959
RTA 97	Bedford SBO	Duple Mid	B40	1954	Jul.1954	Jan.1959
LCV 280	TSM.K6MA7	Theale	C33	1949	Mar.1955	Dec.1958
KJY 204	Commer TS3	Duple	C41	1955	Jun.1955	Jan.1959
KJY 205	Commer TS3	Duple	C41	1955	Jun.1955	Jan.1959
LJY 558	Bedford SBG	Duple	C41	1956	May 1956	May 1958
LJY 584	Commer TS3	Duple	C41	1956	May 1956	Jan.1959
MVA 832	Bedford SBO	Duple Mid	B40	1955	Mar.1957	Jan.1959

Notes:

Vehicles were purchased new unless noted below.

JY 6332, JY 9486 and BCO 510 were acquired from J.W. Newton & Son (Star Motor Service) on the formation of Heybrook Bay Motor Services Ltd in October, 1943.

FHS 486 and MVA 832 were previously operated by Hutchison, Overtown, Scotland.

LCV 280 was previously operated by Stephens, Gunnislake.

PDV 557 passed to Western National on the sale of the business, becoming No. 3825 in that operators fleet.

Livery: Maroon, Red and Cream; later Red and Cream.

Coombes (Plymouth) Ltd. (Princess Tours) — Fleet List 1949 - 1959
Fleet name: Princess Tours

Regn.No.	Make/Model	Body	Seats	New	Acquired	Sold
MMP 808	Bedford OB	Duple	C29	1946	1949	Dec.1958
LOD 533	Bedford OB	Duple	C29	1950	Jul.1950	Jan.1954
NTA 32	Bedford SB	Duple	C33	1951	Aug.1951	Apl.1959

Notes:
MMP 808 was previously operated by Taylor, Caterham.
LOD 533 and NTA 32 were purchased new.

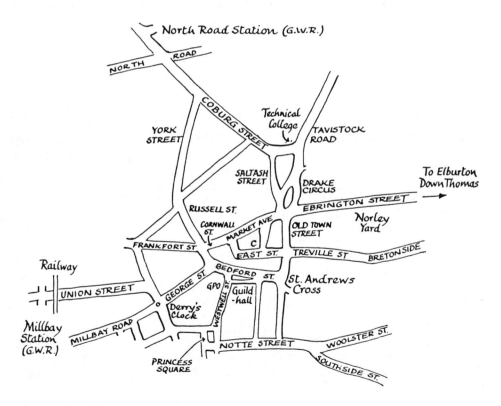

Sketch plan of Plymouth centre showing road layout prior to the post-war reconstruction schemes (C = Corn Exchange)

The fleet in about 1936. On the left of the picture is KP 9701, a Chevrolet, with Bedfords DR 9379 and JY 6332. On the right is Ernie Harwood, the first driver to be employed by Bill Newton.

The first SB model Bedford to join the Heybrook Bay fleet was MOD 541 which had a Duple body and arrived in July 1951.

A line up of Heybrook Bay Motor Services vehicles outside the garage erected by Mr Hart at Down Thomas. From left to right are KJY 204, LJY 584, LJY 558 and XMT 624.

No. 173

No.461545

Certificate of Incorporation

I Hereby Certify, That

COOMBES (PLYMOUTH) LIMITED

is this day Incorporated under the Companies Act, 1948
and that the Company is Limited.

Given under my hand at London this   Twenty-fourth   day of
November   One Thousand Nine Hundred and Forty- eight.

Registrar of Companies.

The certificate of incorporation of Coombes (Plymouth) Ltd

Printed by Kithead Ltd, De Salis Drive, Hampton Lovett, Droitwich Spa, Worcs, WR9 0QE